What If...

The Ideas Never Stopped Flowing

By JanMarie Kelly

What If...

The Ideas Never Stopped Flowing

© JanMarie Kelly

If you would like to use this information in an educational/classroom setting, please first email the publisher at mailto:HarlingHousePublishing@gmail.com

License Notes

JanMarie Kelly
Email: mailto:janmariepublishing@gmail.com
Website: www.janmariekelly.com

HARLING HOUSE

Introduction

The magic words "What If…" can open up a world of writing opportunities and stories for any writer. Keep those words in your mind as you go through your daily life and you will have an endless supply of material from which to draw upon.

The words "What If…" can be used for any type of writing – fiction and nonfiction alike – any genre – any time period. Just take what is before you, say 'what if' and let your mind wander. You may just be surprised at the variety and number of new ideas that start pouring into your mind.

The following pages are filled with "what if" questions asked about normal everyday things – read through a few and see where they take you. I bet it won't take long before you are "what-ifing" all over the place.

It only takes one spark to send you off on a wonderful journey so let's get started…

WHAT IF…

1. … a bus stopped in front of your house (even though there's no bus stop there) and someone different got off each day
2. … a couple could choose who had the baby (the man or woman)
3. … a famous pianist lost his hands in a car accident
4. … a tornado destroyed an entire town, leaving only one church standing in the rubble
5. … actors were paid minimum wage
6. … all animals could disappear and reappear at will
7. … all correspondence was delivered by homing pigeons
8. … all light bulbs came as blue lights
9. … all roads were straight
10. … all scars disappeared within 24 hours

11.   ... all walls were see-through

12.   ... arguments were still decided by dueling

13.   ... average work days were from 2pm to 8pm

14.   ... calendars didn't exist

15.   ... cars could hover above the ground

16.   ... electricity were no longer available to anyone

17.   ... every country was surrounded by impenetrable walls

18.   ... every day were Monday

19.   ... every day were Saturday

20.   ... every room had one wall as a mirror

21.   ... every time you closed your eyes you had a nightmare

22.   ... every time you opened a door it lead to a completely different place

23.   ... everyone carried a key with them on their key ring that when slipped into any computer slot would give a complete, detailed account of that person's life up until that point

24.   ... everyone could read minds

25.   ... everyone could see out of the front AND back of their heads

26.   ... everyone could walk on water

27.   ... everyone got around on snow mobiles

28.   ... everyone had an identical twin

29.   ... everyone had free use of cell phones

30.   ... everyone had the same first name

31.   ... everyone had to attend church service for an hour before work every day

32.   ... everyone had to ride a roller coaster to work

33.   ... everyone had to wear masks out in public

34.   ... everyone knew your name

35.   ... everyone sang to communicate

36.   ... everyone worked in a small cubicle with their bosses watching their every move

37.   ... everything were free and people only had to do what they enjoyed doing

38.   ... hail the size of bowling balls would start falling from the sky

39.   ... humans aged like dogs

40.   ... humans communicated telepathically

41.   ... humans could fly without assistance

42.   ... humans had four arms

43.   ... humans showed affection by punching each other

44.   ... humans were all unisex

45.   ... kissing caused pregnancy

46.   ... light bulbs had never been invented

47.   ... no one had a boss and everyone just went to work, did their part and left

48.   ... no one had to pay any taxes any more

49.   ... physical books were extinct

50.   ... placing your hand over any area that was in pain on your body would remove the pain instantly

51.   ... printers made their own paper and ink as needed

52.   ... Siamese twins automatically broke apart at age two

53.   ... someone on a plane full of people suddenly released a deadly virus

54.   ... the calendar year consisted of 18 months instead of 12

55.   ... the military was the highest paying profession

56.   ... there was a celebrated holiday every week of the year

57.　　　... there were a little flaming dragon inside of your oven that cooked your food

58.　　　... there were no drive-through restaurants

59.　　　... there were no forms of birth control

60.　　　... there were no mirrors

61.　　　... there were no more physical mail

62.　　　... time started moving backwards

63.　　　... to discard a piece of paper all you had to do was crumple it up into a ball and throw it in the air

64.　　　... vehicles did not have headlights

65.　　　... vehicles ran on solar power

66.　　　... whatever you thought - materialized before you

67.　　　... while doing research on the internet you stumbled on to what looked like a live feed into someone's living room

68.　　　... while driving home one night you passed a person lying alongside the road

69.   ... while playing the board game Risk (a war game) you ended up right in the middle of your war in real time

70.   ... while working late one night, you witnessed a theft

71.   ... you could automatically tell whenever someone was lying

72.   ... you could choose any job to be your career and you would automatically have all the knowledge necessary for it on your first day

73.   ... you could draw the kind of house you wanted, lay that paper in the area of the ground you wanted your house, stand back and clap your hands twice and that very house would appear

74.   ... you could only get pregnant between the ages of 25-30

75.   ... you could place your hand on a wall and hear what was happening on the other side

76.	... you could stop time at will

77.	... you could think about what you would like to have for super and when you got home it would be prepared and waiting for you

78.	... you could throw your papers into the air and they would automatically be filed in the proper places

79.	... you could transfer your pain onto anyone else you chose

80.	... you couldn't stop talking for 24 hours straight

81.	... you felt like you were being watched/followed

82.	... you got to work and someone completely different showed up as your boss

83.	... you had to make a public speech every time you wanted to request time off of work

84.   ... you had to work ten hour days with no breaks

85.   ... you had to work, ten hours a day, everyday for the government and they provided your food & housing in return, but if you didn't work you didn't get your food for that day

86.   ... you kept hearing footsteps in your house, but could not find anyone in any of the rooms

87.   ... you never had to change the oil in your car

88.   ... you only needed to stick your finger in the middle of your food to cook it to perfect temperature

89.   ... you pick up your phone at home to make a call and hear a conversation going on

90.   ... you showed up at work and they were doing mandatory drug testing -- yours came back positive even though you

know you haven't taken so much as an aspirig

91.   ... you stopped at a corner store on your way home and walked right into the middle of a robbery

92.   ... you turned on the news and it was just a shot of an empty newsroom on your tv

93.   ... you were face to face with the person who had just conned you out of your life's savings, what would you do

94.   ... you were locked out of your house in the middle of a winter storm

95.   ... you were typing away on your work computer and suddenly smelled something burning

96.   ... you were unable to tell the truth

97.   ... you witnessed a murder

98.   ... you woke up one morning and had no idea who you were or where you were

99.   ... you worked a different job every day

100.   ... your bank account balance never went below 10,000 dollars - no matter how much you spent each day

101.   ... your personal assistant was spying on you and reporting things about you to a government agency

102.   ... a cat ran into your house when you opened the front door to leave for work

103.   ... all taxes doubled overnight

104.   ... everyone worked overnight

105.   ... everything tasted like chocolate

106.   ... people could only communicate with each other through writing

107.   ... while attending the funeral of a well-known government official, shots rang out

108.　… while you were attending the funeral of a close friend, you heard something move within the coffin

109.　… you bought a house that was filled with secret passage ways you knew nothing about

110.　… you came face to face with a ruthless dictator

111.　… you were asked to be 'Dear Abby' for a week

112.　… you were given a column in the Sunday edition of a nationally read newspaper to write about anything you wanted, what would you write about

113.　… a bear showed up rooting through your garbage

114.　… a dangerous prisoner escaped from the local prison and you lived alone

115.　… a gang moved in to your neighborhood and started threatening everyone

116.　… a huge storm suddenly appeared and you had a party of 50 in your backyard

117.　… a man was found hanging in a tree in the park behind your apartment building

118.　… a motorcycle gang moved in next door

119.　… a moving truck was in your driveway when you woke up

120.　… a mysterious couple moved in next door to you

121.　… a stranger pulled into your driveway and didn't get out of his car

122.　… all animals were domesticated

123.　… all boundaries were strictly enforced

124.　… all houses were made of glass

125.　… all marine life could walk and live on land

126. … all of the furniture you had and used was gliding/swinging furniture

127. … all planets were inhabited

128. … all plant life provided healthy, delicious edible food (and it was all free)

129. … all vehicles were the exact same make, model and color

130. … all water sources were only ten feet deep

131. … all your neighbors moved away and you were the only one left in your town

132. … children came by mail delivery instead of the birthing process

133. … clothes were optional, everywhere

134. … days were 48 hours long

135. … dogs only ate humans

136. … dogs were our masters

137. … during a neighborhood cookout someone pulls a gun and grabs a hostage

138.   … elevator music constantly played everywhere you went

139.   … every family had ten or more children

140.   … everyone around you spoke a language you didn't understand

141.   … everyone built their own homes

142.   … everyone carried a gun/weapon

143.   … everyone cooked their meals outside

144.   … everyone had a high IQ

145.   … everyone had to grow their own food

146.   … everyone had to serve in their country's military for two years

147.   … everyone had to start working at the age of ten

148.   … everyone lived in apartments and there were no houses

149.   … everyone lived outside

150.　　… everyone started their day with exercise

151.　　… everyone worked for themselves

152.　　… everyone's property were fenced in (electric fences?)

153.　　… fish swam in the air and birds soared underwater

154.　　… food lost all its flavor

155.　　… food were free to everyone

156.　　… guns and bombs/explosives were never made

157.　　… horses were allowed to roam free

158.　　… houses had no windows

159.　　… humans could hear what dogs heard

160.　　… humans didn't have the capacity to hear

161.　　… humans lived to be 500 years old

162.　　… humans were afraid of water

163.　… humans were reborn after death into another family

164.　… it hadn't rained in your town in over 3 months

165.　… it only rained at night while everyone was sleeping

166.　… it rained 365 days a year

167.　… it was always the perfect temperature and we didn't need heat or air conditioning

168.　… life never ended

169.　… life was a silent movie

170.　… lightning split the tree in front of your house

171.　… meat were no longer an option for food

172.　… medicine hadn't advanced

173.　… no humans knew how to swim

174.　… no one had a high IQ

175.　… no one had to lock their doors

176.   … no one was allowed to sue anyone else

177.   … no one were allowed to have animals as pets

178.   … no one wore shoes

179.   … no vehicles were allowed within city limits

180.   … paper money did not exist

181.   … people just showed up at your door, unannounced

182.   … people needed 12 hours of sleep

183.   … people only needed 2 hours of sleep

184.   … rain came up from the ground instead of down from the sky

185.   … rainbows really did have a pot of gold at the end of them

186.   … science didn't exist

187.   … she never came back

188.   … someone cut you off and made you have an accident

189.   … someone wrote about your life without your consent and filled the book with lies

190.   … temperatures were always in the 100's

191.   … the active and lively woods you lived in suddenly became very still and silent

192.   … the air always smelled like homemade apple pie

193.   … the big oak tree in your back yard was in a different spot when you came home

194.   … the creek in your back yard grew into the size of a small river overnight

195.   … the dreams you had at night came true the next day

196.   … the economy collapsed and everyone in town knew you had stashed supplies

197.　　… the escalator you were riding up in suddenly started moving backwards, quickly

198.　　… the garage you took your car to, lost your car

199.　　… the garbage men skipped your house two weeks in a row

200.　　… the ground you were walking on started to split apart

201.　　… the house you were house sitting at, burnt to the ground

202.　　… the house you were house sitting at, got robbed

203.　　… the leaves on trees were always brilliant colors instead of green

204.　　… the news was broadcasted over loud speakers

205.　　… the oceans started boiling

206.　　… the only job you could get was a cook at an Indian restaurant and you knew nothing about Indian food

207.   … the only way to get the latest news was to show up for the nightly meeting at the town square

208.   … the police raided your home

209.   … the puppy you were watching, ran away

210.   … the sun good piecre through trees and there was no longer any shade

211.   … the weather man reported rough waters and extremely high winds for the lake area, which was 50 yards from your house

212.   … the work week was two days long and the weekends were five days long

213.   … there was a dog barking constantly at the next door neighbor's house that you found to be abandoned

214.   … there was never another moment of silence

215.   … there was never any darkness

216.   ... there was only one nationality in the world

217.   ... there were a species bigger and smarter than humans that started taking over our homes

218.   ... there were dueling gods of equal powering fighting for control of the earth

219.   ... there were no airplanes

220.   ... there were no babies, humans started at the age of five

221.   ... there were no boundaries, anywhere

222.   ... there were no cemeteries

223.   ... there were no federal government and each state had their own laws with no outside authority

224.   ... there were no garbage

225.   ... there were no garbage service

226.   ... there were no governments

227.   ... there were no hate in the world

228.   ... there were no love in the world

229.　　… there were no more grocery stores

230.　　… there were no mountains and valleys, but all land was flat

231.　　… there were no paved roads

232.　　… there were no religion

233.　　… they build a super max prison ½ a mile from your home

234.　　… travel between planets were as common as travel between states

235.　　… two dogs started fighting right in front of you

236.　　… vehicles could not go more than twenty miles per hour

237.　　… when you came out to the garage after work, your car was missing

238.　　… when you were done shopping in a big, strange city you couldn't find your car

239.　　… while at your friend's house the phone started ringing and your friend, with a look of terror on her face, refused to answer it

240. ... while driving home late one night you noticed someone following you

241. ... while making your significant other a special home cooked meal, your stove burst into flames

242. ... while showering the water turned blood red

243. ... while stopped at a red light you were propositioned by a hooker

244. ... wild animals roamed the streets freely

245. ... winter lasted all year long

246. ... you accidentally cut someone off and now they were following you

247. ... you are not entitled to a lawyer and can be tried without one

248. ... you came home and found you had been robbed

249.   … you could choose to see things in black and white or color

250.   … you could never get enough to eat

251.   … you couldn't go out into the sun

252.   … you felt an energy shift in your home after one of the occupants went away on a trip

253.   … you found a mysterious panel to a hidden passageway in a home you just bought

254.   … you found a note on your refrigerator in the morning, but no one else lived with you

255.   … you found a strange dog in the dog pen with your dogs

256.   … you got fired

257.   … you had a bbq and one of your guest died

258.   … you had no family or friends to call on for help/support

259.   … you had no phone service and you were sure someone was breaking into your house

260.   … you had to get around on all fours

261.   … you had to learn to barter for all your needs

262.   … you had to provide everything for yourself

263.   … you had to repair your own vehicle to get to safety

264.   … you heard a faint cry in the distance

265.   … you heard a strange noise coming from inside your tub's drain

266.   … you heard music playing faintly in the background, but were the only one home

267.   … you heard screams in the building across the street from your apartment

268.   … you heard the voice of you dead grandmother while you were alone in your home at night

269.   … you held a neighborhood yard sale and no one showed up

270.   … you looked out your window only to see a cow grazing in your backyard

271.   … you lost your ability to speak

272.   … you needed blood to survive

273.   … you needed ID and a key card to go anywhere (into stores, into work, into post office, etc.)

274.   … you never were hungry again

275.   … you noticed you forgot to turn the oven on and your boss will be arriving in ten minutes to eat

276.   … you saw a kidnapping but no one would believe you

277.   … you saw the world in monochrome

278.　　… you smelled smoke in the air, but couldn't see any

279.　　… you smelled something electrical burning, but couldn't find its source

280.　　… you stripped all your clothes off at work and ran from the building

281.　　… you threw a party for your son and your expensive jewelry ended up missing

282.　　… you took your dogs for a walk and got lost

283.　　… you went in to work and no one there was familiar to you

284.　　… you went to work one morning and the building was empty

285.　　… you were asked to report on the tragedy happening in your neighborhood for your local news

286.　　… you were driving into work and noticed there was no one else on the road during rush hour

287.　… you were driving to work but ended up somewhere else

288.　… you were forced to move within 24 hours

289.　… you were forced to murder someone to save your child

290.　… you were never able to sleep again

291.　… you were promoted to a position you've always wanted, but had to move to another country

292.　… you were sent on a scavenger hunt where your life was dependent upon your success

293.　… you were the only human who could breathe under water

294.　… you were trapped alone in a high rise elevator

295.　… you were trapped with a claustrophobic inside an elevator

296.   … you woke up in a different house then the one you went to slip in

297.   … you woke up in a strange/different neighborhood

298.   … you won the lottery but weren't allowed to spend any of it on anyone but yourself

299.   … you won the lottery but weren't allowed to spend any of it on yourself

300.   … you wrote about the perfect murder and then someone used it to commit murder of someone you know

301.   … your accountant stole all your money and made it look like you committed fraud

302.   … your car drove itself

303.   … your cat started talking to you in a language you understood

304.   … your daughter got caught shoplifting

305.　… your dentist broke off a drill bit in your mouth

306.　… your doctor removed a perfectly healthy limb of yours

307.　… your dog went missing (or a dog you were watching went missing)

308.　… your every movement was watched and recorded

309.　… your generator exploded while it was going through a test run

310.　… your house caught fire while you were asleep

311.　… your house could communicate with you

312.　… your house was totally automated, but malfunctioned and you were stuck inside

313.　… your lawyer committed the crime you are being accused of

314.　… your neighbor ended up dead on your property

315. ... your neighbor offered to buy your property for three times what it was worth

316. ... your neighbor offered to sell his land to you for ¼ of what it was worth

317. ... your neighbor suddenly went missing

318. ... your neighbor were elderly and ill and had no one to care for her

319. ... your neighbor's house burnt down and you believed your son was responsible

320. ... your neighborhood was having a block party and everyone was invited but you

321. ... your neighbors started mysteriously disappearing, one by one

322. ... your neighbors were planning to overtake your house and kill you

323. ... your new neighbor had a vicious dog that kept getting loose

324. … your only mode of transportation was a bicycle

325. … your only mode of transportation was walking

326. … your savings all disappeared

327. … your septic tank cracked and the sewage leaked out all over your yard

328. … your son were arrested for murder and you were unsure of his innocence

329. … your toilet were overflowing and you could not turn off the water

330. … your tomatoes out produced your ability to harvest and make use of them

331. … your yard was full of different sizes and shapes of balls when you went out in the morning

332. … a group of cats showed up on your porch one morning

333.   … the business where you dropped your computer off to get repaired was no longer there when you went back to pick it up

334.   … the generator failed during a lengthy 'black-out' in your town (in the dead of winter – in the middle of summer)

335.   … you couldn't pay the taxes on your land/home

336.   … you were sent to the bank by your boss to make a deposit and while they it got robbed

337.   … your garden produce started disappearing

338.   … your well water was contaminated by a new plant in town

339.   … the deck you were standing on started to give way

340.   … the small garden you planted started to take over your yard

341.	… the overhead fan came loose and flew around the room

342.	… your fish outgrew their aquarium

343.	… the company you worked for became a segregated building

344.	… every time you woke up it was in a different, unfamiliar place

345.	… you could immediately become an expert in any field you chose

346.	… insects were 1000 times bigger than they are now

347.	… humans hair grew a foot a day

348.	… you could make up a new genre, what would it be

349.	… humans lived with the animals

350.	… plants lived on oxygen

351.	… having your picture taken really did steal your sole

352.	… music were constantly playing in the background

353.   … each season lasted only a week at a time

354.   … regular work hours were from 10pm to 6am

355.   … regular business days lasted for twelve hours each

356.   … every worker were entitled to eight weeks of vacation every year

357.   … men wore the dresses

358.   … all schools had uniforms for their students

359.   … schools were in session year round

360.   … there were only one universal language

361.   … all children were home schooled

362.   … all college courses were taken online

363.   … colleges no longer existed

364.   … grass came in multiple colors

365.   … you are a detective who must make it to a building in the city by 5pm, but you hit heavy traffic that threatens to make you late

Bonus Section:

What If…
  - turtles were the dominant species

  - every family had five acres to live on

  - people walked around on all fours

  - the 'work week' consisted of two days and the rest was time off

  - the 'work day' was from noon to five

  - everyone had to barter for their goods and services

  - music was never invented

  - electricity was never discovered

  - it snowed all year round – everywhere

  - it were sunny and in the 70's all year round – everywhere

  - there were only one race of people

  - everyone spoke the same language

- we could easily travel to other planets

- we knew there was life on other planets and could communicate with them

- you didn't need any type of vehicle to travel and could just 'think' yourself there

- you could use your mind to do, be or have anything

- it were daytime all the time --- everywhere

- it were nighttime all the time --- everywhere

- we only needed an hour sleep as a species

- we only had cold water

- our bodies transformed according to the weather – heavy fur in the winter, light skin with sun protection in the summer, etc.

- people didn't live in house, but slept under the open sky

- you are home alone at night, someone knocks on your door & when you go to look no one is there – then you hear knocking on a back window, again, no one is there

- if your spouse winds up dead in your home after the neighbors heard a big argument the night before and you have no alibi for the time of death

- there have been numerous break-ins in your neighborhood and the town is accusing your child

- you spent years writing books to build a catalogue and suddenly no one read any more

- people were like chameleons and could blend into their surroundings

- public transportation were non-existent

- you were on a crowded bus in the middle of a large city when it came under attack from fighter planes

- you could understand the thoughts and feelings of any living thing in your presence

- restaurants didn't exist

- grocery stores didn't exist and everyone had to grow and store their own food

- grocery stores didn't exist and everyone had to eat out

- what if people could just pass through walls and doors and windows weren't necessary

- there were only one time zone

- every city were on a different time zone

- there were no colors in the world – only black and white

- people changed color depending on their mood

- humans didn't start working until they were in their fifties

- every person had a chip implanted at birth that could tell the government all their information, including their location at any time

- you could take a photo of any face and transpose that face onto yours

- you could change your body shape and size at will

- all people had hand to hand combat training

- all people carried weapons with them wherever they went

- the world had one ruler and countries could no longer decide their own laws

- electronics where never invented

- in the blink of an eye everyone was transferred back to the 1800's, but only had the knowledge and skill sets they had in the 21st century

- eating chocolate made people violently ill or killed them like it does with some animals

- humans went from baby to adult in 5 years instead of 18

- humans went from baby to adult in 30 years instead of 18

- dogs lived for 40 years

- nothing ever died

- paper were never invented

- everything were electronic and there were no hard copies of anything

- you came home late one night, alone, and saw flashlights moving around inside your home

- you came home from work and found your large family of ten had disappeared without a trace

- humans slept standing up

- dishes washed themselves

- you could just turn a knob to adjust the height of your grass and never had to mow again

- it rained every day

- dogs had two arms and two legs like humans

- you only had to plant your vegetable garden once and then it just continually produced year after year

- your body used everything it took in and there was never any waste to get rid of

- every house had a treadmill and you were required to clock an hour on it every day

- all animals were vegetarian and nothing ate meat

- all animals were carnivores and only ate meat

- there were no court systems and everyone just handled things themselves

- when you moved to a new home you could just clap and all of your belongings and furnishings would just appear in the new home

- the only way you could cook anything was over and open fire

- you found out you were pregnant, but new you were a virgin

- men got pregnant

- humans laid eggs

- houses could be built in a day

- you could draw on a piece of paper the item you wanted, tap on the picture and it became real

- people and animals lived among each other with no barriers

- everyone could read minds

- when you traveled you didn't need to carry any luggage – it just showed up at your destination

- sports didn't exist

- being in the military paid more than being a movie star

- movie starts got paid minimum wage

- colleges didn't exist

- the only education you received was from your family and life experiences

- all houses were limited to 500 square feet

- every home had a pool

- there were no swimming pools – anywhere

- the main source of transportation were hovercrafts

- you didn't need a license to drive

- there were no such thing as identification and you could use whatever name you wanted and change it at will

- no passports were needed to travel internationally

- you didn't need umbrellas, but could walk around, no matter what the weather, without getting wet

- people lived on the water instead of land

- history books and stories didn't exist and you had no clue as to what happened in times gone by

- when you cut a tree down the stump would automatically, and quickly, grow a new tree

- no cleaning supplies were ever needed again – you would just wave your hand and the space you were in became spotless and clutter free

- there were no stores and you had to make the things you wanted and needed

- you got paid only once a year

- whatever you visualized became reality

- homes could never burn down

- once people hit forty they never got any older

- every household had a personal cook

- the US Congress got paid minimum wage

- all people were Libertarian and everyone could do as they pleased with their lives so long as they didn't harm another (did not say didn't offend another – said didn't harm another)

- marriage didn't exist and everyone just lived with whomever they wanted, as long as they wanted

- children had to start working at ten years old

- everyone lived alone

- there were only one gender

- you got into a car accident in the middle of nowhere and when the guy in the other car got out you recognized him as the serial killer that the FBI has been hunting

- everyone were bald

- everyone had to serve five years in their countries military

- you were working late at the office when the power went out

- you went to work at your big office building an no one else showed up

- you then looked outside and the streets were bare

- after showering people just 'shook dry' like dogs do

- we had no sense of smell

- you were out digging in your garden and you came across a buried metal box

- humans had eyes in both the front and back of their head

- plants used oxygen instead of carbon dioxide

- humans lived underwater

- you woke up in a foreign country where you didn't speak the language

- your cruise ship were hijacked by pirates

- escaped convicts overtook your home

- your office building were on lock down with a terrorist running loose inside

- your country asked you to be a spy for national security

- you lost both your legs in an automobile accident

- everyone needed wheelchairs to get around

- you were held hostage inside a bank

- you accidentally got locked in a bank vault

- you were locked inside a mall overnight

- mall security were chasing a shoplifter down the mall and the thief ran smack into you

- you heard about a car chase on the highway you were driving on and then suddenly saw the car speeding towards you in your rear view mirror

- everyone had chauffeurs

- everyone had a body guard

- everyone had an arranged marriage

- everyone were allowed to have only one child

- it were mandatory that everyone use grills to cook their food during the summer

- your boss asked you to do something illegal

- your boss threatened to turn you in for embezzlement unless you did as he asked

- every family had ten pets

- no one were allowed to have pets

- people were kept in zoos

- everyone changed careers every five years

- everyone had a different job each year

- you grew a completely original vegetable in your garden and the government came to investigate

- helicopters could be called and used like a taxi service

- everyone were called by their last names and no one had a first name

- everyone had to wear headphones to be able to hear

- you got paid to watch you tube videos

- you got paid to sleep

- dessert was eaten first at meals

➢ you could turn any food you were served, that you didn't like, into your favorite food

➢ everyone sang their conversations instead of talked

➢ you were offered 10,000 dollars to hit someone with your car

➢ you were approached by the FBI to spy on your boss

➢ you worked on a road crew that was working on a bridge and you suddenly felt the bridge give way

➢ you were stuck in an elevator alone in a high rise building

➢ a co-worker got into a shouting match with her boss right in front of your desk

➢ you're sitting at your desk and work and you hear something rattling around in the ceiling above your desk

➢ you come into work and all your personal belongings are packed up in a box

➢ you were at work and couldn't keep from drifting off to sleep

➢ you stopped at the corner store for your morning coffee and it got robbed while you were inside

➢ you bought the latest 'best-seller' and as you started reading you discovered it was exactly like the manuscript you had written years before

➢ you woke up and the grass was blue and the sky was green

➢ when you look out the window you see your house is floating in the air. You looked around and noticed all the houses on your block were also floating

➢ the elevators doors opened and as you walked out you were knocked out by a blow to the head

➢ clocks went in a counter-clockwise position

➢ all humans had bright red skin

➢ dogs were the 'masters' and people the pets

- every home had at least one gun

- guns were never invented

- abortions were not physically possible

- there were no news media

- there were no individual countries

- everyone had to have at least a small garden

- grocery stores didn't exist

- everyone worked from home

- electricity hadn't been invented
- your mother called to tell you she was leaving the country never to return

- people only had one eye and it was located on their chins

- your small backyard morphed into a 200 acre forest

- you left your office building only to find you were in an unfamiliar city

- you just stocked your refrigerator and freezer and the hurricane knocked out all of the power

- you were driving home from your weekend trip and a torrential downpour washed out the road in front of you

- you were vacationing just miles from a volcano when it decided to erupt

- the snow storm that was supposed to end in 48 hours was still going strong after five days

- a week long snow storm dumped so much snow that it caved in your roof

- your house cat morphed into a tiger

- you came home to find a bear cub on your porch

- the raccoon that had been raiding your trash, started picking up after himself

- you woke up to the headline "President Disappears"

- the doctor just told you were pregnant, and you're a male

- you woke up 100 pounds heavier than you were when you went to bed last night

- you were in the middle of an important speech and all your teeth started to fall out

- you had just jumped out of the plane for your first solo skydive and your arms no longer worked

- our bodies did not need any sleep to be highly functional

- everyone had to use sign language to communicate

- clocks went from 1 to 24

- there were 48 hours in a day

- when you left your house for work in the morning the entire sky was bright orange

- what if we only saw in black and white and shades of gray

- there were only one breed of dog

- every household had two or more pets

- no one were allowed to have pets

- you were allowed to take your dog everywhere with you

- the only transportation was public buses

- there were human communities on five of our other planets and transportation to and from each planet

- you could invent something the whole world would buy – what would it be

- you could only ever eat 5 different food items for the rest of your life – which 5 food items would you pick

- you stumbled upon a real-live working time machine – would you use it – which time period would you go to

- you were given the chance to relive one day of your life over again – which day would you choose

- you could go back and choose one year of your life to 'redo' – which year would you choose and why

- you could snap your fingers and be transported to any place in the world that you were thinking of

- people didn't start working until their 30's – what would you do with those extra 'free' years

- you could choose any career you wanted, stick a chip in your brain and automatically have the skills & knowledge for that career

- you saw someone shoplifting

- you were trapped in a bank while it was being robbed

- you saw someone being killed and the murderer saw you

- everyone could have one artistic talent – which would you choose

- you hit a parked car and were sure no one saw you do it – what would you do

- you went to the bank to cash a check and the teller gave you back 1,000 dollars instead of 100

- you found a large manila envelope in the street and when you looked inside it was stuffed full of cash

- you found a wallet with ID and a large amount of money

- you saw a baby locked in a car on a hot day – what would you do

- you saw a dog locked in a car on a hot day – what would you do

- if your best friend's significant other hit on you

- if you caught your best friend's significant other cheating

- you never failed at anything you did

- humans only lived to be 40 – what would you do differently

- the only way to get goods or services was to do a kind deed

- a loved one was in serious trouble, but the only way to help them included breaking the law – would you

- your country were in total collapse & you had to move to another country to survive – which country do you choose

- you got on the elevator at work, pushed the 10th floor, but the elevator kept going and didn't stop until it got to the 22nd floor – your building only has 16 floors

- you had to pick between losing all of your past memories or never being able to create any new ones – which would you choose

- your greatest fear came true

- there were no religions in the world

- everyone believed in the same religion

- you could be remembered for anything – whether it were true or not – what would you choose to be remembered for

- what you consider reality is really just one big dream

- you could write your life story before it happened – what would you write

- all Gods really do exist

- fear did not exist

- you could change your physical appearance each day like you do your clothes

- school lasted for 10 hours a day, 6 days a week, 12 months a year

- you could get a great night's sleep every single night and wake up re-energized and happy every morning, but in order to do so you would have to sleep alone for the remainder of your life

- you could make 50,000 a year, but you would have to clean public restrooms to get it

- you could control your dreams by stating what you wanted to dream about before you went to bed

- you were given this one of a kind printer that could print real money

- you could have any job in the world, what job would you choose

- you could take a month long trip to another planet – would you go – and which planet would you like to go to

- you could get a job as a sport's mascot – would you accept – and which mascot would you like to be

- you could telecommute and only had to physically go to your job once a week

- a private company successfully drilled to the core of the earth and offered you a ride to the center – would you go

- there were no such thing as gravity

- your new job offered 6 weeks of vacation every year, but you had to work 12 hour days, 6 days a week the rest of the year – would you

- your boss asked you to do something that you did not agree with, but that was neither immoral nor illegal – would you do it

- you were offered the opportunity to go back to school – all fees paid – would you and what courses would you take

- you didn't have to work and could spend all of your time on a worthwhile cause, a hobby, or a passion – what would you choose to spend your time on

- the south had actually won the US Civil War – how would things be different

- Germany won World War II

- President Abe Lincoln were not assassinated

- the Federal Reserve were never created

- American presidents could run for unlimited terms

- all American schools were run privately

- all American children were home schooled

- corporal punishment remained in full force at all of our schools

- capital punishment was strictly enforced in all states

- the US had no court system and vigilante justice was the only way to get any justice at all

- the internet didn't exist

- every household in the world had free internet access

- cigarettes were never invented

- there were no drugs (good or bad) in the world

- every country had access to nuclear energy and weapons

- marriage didn't exist and people just lived together as they saw fit

- it was illegal to live together unless you were married

- there were no houses and everyone just lived in big multi-unit buildings

- everyone had to take a half hour exercise break at their jobs each day

- everyone lived to be at least 200 years old before getting sickly and/or dying

- there were no patents or copyrights and anyone could copy anything they wanted from anyone else

- every day was 100 degrees or hotter

- every day were zero degrees or colder

- all people were born deaf

- every time you put money in the bank it would be doubled the next day

- donuts, cakes and pies were health food

- all the claims in the bible are true

- during your first year at a prestigious college you failed every single class

- television were never invented

- every person had to serve in the country's military for at least 2 years

- humans were all one color

- humans were all different colors like a pack of crayons

- humans lived in the wild like all other animals

- hundreds of cats just roamed freely throughout your town
- you could work whichever hours and whichever days you wanted to as long as you worked 32 hours every week

- ➢ your neighbors partied all night long every night of the week

- ➢ you heard screams coming from your neighbor's house late one night and then you never saw the female of the house again after that night

- ➢ you witnessed your neighbor burning a large burn pile in his back yard with a foul smell and you hadn't seen his wife in a while

- ➢ you heard moaning coming from your basement late at night while you were home alone

- ➢ the sounds of sirens woke you up in the middle of the night and you looked at the window only to see your neighbor's house surrounded by cops

- ➢ the city bus you rode every morning to work were hijacked

- ➢ the city bus you rode to work every morning were in a 5 vehicle pile up

- fire didn't exist

- everyone still traveled by horseback

- you had to kill the animals yourself in order to eat

- humans did not eat meat

- you were trapped on the 16th floor of your office building when a raging fire broke out on the 5th floor

- you were walking along city streets and you heard gun fire – what if you had children with you at the time

- you were at work and a group of masked gun men stormed through the front doors

- the person you see in the mirror is not actually what you look like

- everyone sees a different person when they look at you

- there really is life on other planets and they consider our spacecraft UFO's and us aliens

- you didn't need any special suits to travel in space

- there were floating cities that just bobbed around in the ocean

- ghosts were real and everyone could easily communicate with them

- you didn't really die, but transformed into a spirit and could still maintain contact with your family and friends

- work weeks consisted of 5 days and the weekend also consisted of 5 days making our weeks 10 days long

- everything that you touched turned to whatever you were thinking about at the time you touched it

- everyone had pet lions

- wolves were harmless and ran free in all neighborhoods

- a year consisted of 1200 days

- everyone were paid daily for their work

- there were not taxes – on anything

- there were no minimum wage

- every time you were asked to do something you had never done before you were automatically given the knowledge needed to do the task

- hate were nonexistent

- evil did not exist

- a murder a week were committed in your town

- everyone had to wear black and white clothing and there were no colored clothes to be found anywhere

- everyone had the same haircuts

- glasses and contact lenses were never invented

- cow really did give chocolate and strawberry milk

- everyone had a cow or goat and that is where they got their own milk

- you could design your baby on the computer and have it mailed to you (no pregnancy, delivery, or hospital stay needed)

- everyone had an implant in their ear that they could just click on, say a name and it would call whoever they wanted

- calendars didn't exist and you never knew what day, month or year it was

- humans could only see in the dark

- every kid really did have 'imaginary' friends and they kept them into adulthood

- you woke up in a room you didn't recognize

- you rolled over in your bed in the morning and saw someone you did not know lying beside you

- the person lying beside you, in an unfamiliar bed, were dead

- you woke up covered in blood

- you woke up in your house in the morning, got ready for work, but when you left the house you were in an unfamiliar town

- your dog followed you to work

- when you woke up you have forgotten how to speak English (or your native language)

- your employer moved to another country and you could move there and keep your job or stay where you were and lose your job

- you lose your job only to never be able to find another job

- you quit your lucrative job to start your dream business and that business fails within the first year

- you spend your 'emergency money' on a trip of a lifetime only to come home and find that the roof on your home has collapsed and you have no money to repair it

- a bike was your only means of transportation and it got stolen while you were in the store getting groceries

- governments started making people pay for air

- all water had to be bought

- babies were implanted with chips that could track their location at all times

- a government agent came to your house once a week to do a home inspection

- guns were illegal and only the government's police force were allowed to own/operate any weapons

- nap times were offered at all places of employment

- you were sure your mail carrier was a spy

- you went to a co-workers desk to ask them a question and they were sleeping on their desk

- all clowns were axe murderers

- you walked into a restaurant that was usually packed during the day and there was no one in sight

- you've been sending texts to all your family and friends all day long and no one has responded

- clouds were rainbow colors

- the president of the US were captured by an enemy country

- your country was forced to learn an entirely new language

- you decided to raise chickens and they didn't stop growing

- a bomb went off at your neighbor's house

- you forget to pick up your kids from school

- you come home and your front door is standing wide open

- everyone in your neighborhood has been robbed, but you

- your house keeps getting robbed, month after month

- the earth suddenly had 5 moons

- the earth moved closer to the sun every year

- people's noses grew, like Pinocchio's nose, every time they lied

- we could step into our televisions and be an actual part of our favorite shows

- you woke up as someone different every day of your life

- boxing matches were to the death

- all men wore dresses and had long hair

- the night before your wedding you find out your fiancée has gone missing

- you found out the person you had been flirting with on the bus turned out to be a serial killer

- the train you rode to work every day suddenly jumped the tracks one morning

- smoking were still allowed at work desks and in all office buildings

- you were asked to forge your boss' signature

- a very embarrassing secret of yours was about to become public

- someone tried blackmailing you

- you had a juicy secret about your boss that you could use to your advantage

- your boss made sexual advances towards you

➢ an office flirtation suddenly became serious

➢ the helicopter that dropped off the CEO of your company every day, lost power and slammed into the roof of your building

➢ fast food restaurants did not exist

➢ all food tasted the same

➢ prisons really did only serve bread and water to the inmates

➢ they still had "chain gangs" throughout all the states

➢ athletes were only paid median wages

➢ actors were only paid 40 grand a year

➢ everyone lived on house boats

➢ animals took over the land and humans were forced to the sea

➢ your neighbor, who has been out on a worker's comp disability for a year, was in the backyard jumping on the trampoline with his child

- you knew of someone who was seriously cheating on their taxes – would you turn them in to collect the reward

- the government asked you to spy on your neighbors – would you

- you were lying on your death bed and given 48 hours to make your peace – who would you talk to and what would you say

- you were driving down a part of town you don't usually visit and saw your spouse's vehicle outside of a motel room

- you see a police officer shoot an unarmed kid who was just walking along the street

- you saw a police officer get shot and the criminal took off down the alley

- you saw someone beating up a cop – would you intervene

- a car crashes into your local grocery store, but when the fire is put out no body is found

- you could fake your own death and get away with it – would you

- your friend asks you to pick up his lotter ticket because he has to work late then he never shows up to get the ticket – his numbers come in and he wins a million dollars – do you give him the ticket, ask to share or claim it as your own

- your boss came to work drunk every day – what if it were a co-worker instead

- your sibling robbed a bank and came to you for a place to hide – do you hide them or turn them in

- your son commits murder – do you try to talk him into turning himself in, turn him in yourself, or not say anything to anyone

- you had one hour to be invisible – what would you do and where would you go

- you were a mid-level accountant for what you thought was a legitimate company until the police raid – what do you do when you are swept up on the investigation

- ➤ you are being investigated for a murder you did not commit, of someone you didn't even know – the evidence against you is pretty strong – what do you do

- ➤ every time you lie you involuntarily scream LIAR

- ➤ when you are 30 years old your parents tell you that you were adopted and they don't know who your biological parents are

- ➤ you have stumbled on to a small town that murders any outsiders that stay too long

- ➤ you had to interview your boss' replacement

- ➤ after turning down a proposal of marriage from a guy you had been dating for 6 months, you found out he came from an extremely wealthy family

- you are awaken at night by all the lights and televisions in your house turning on at once

- you are talking on the phone and it goes dead – then the lights go out – then you hear footsteps down the hall

- a friend you have allowed to 'crash for a couple of days' on your couch has now been there for over a month

- houses had no windows and doors – just openings

- you could choose what happened to you when you die – what 'afterlife' would you choose

- you found an animal that was supposed to be extinct

- you had the opportunity to either skip ahead 5 years or go back 5 years – which do you choose and why

- humans didn't need to go to the bathroom and instead they just 'sweat out' their waste

- you have been ordered to kill someone close to your or you will be killed a long, slow death – what do you do

- you were asked to join a neighborhood group to rid your town of the drug dealers – do you join – what does the group do

- your high school nemesis calls you up and wants to get together for lunch – do you go – what could they want – what happens

- you had lost the last $20 that you had and your kids were hungry – what would you do

- all land were flat prairies

- you were grabbed in the middle of the night, blind-folded and walked barefoot through the woods behind your house

- you could summon rain or sun at will – what would you do with this power

- while spying on someone and taking their photo they see you

- you are murdered but come back as a ghost – do you haunt the person that murdered you or spend your time being close with your family

- you witnessed an old lady in the process of being mugged

- you overhear a co-worker planning to steal from the employer you both work for

- one of your children decided they wanted to join a cult

- when you get on the elevator at work to go home it keeps going down further and further past the basement level of your building – what happens when it finally stops and the doors open

- you had to break into your own home – how would you do it and why was it necessary

- you were sent to prison for a crime you didn't commit and the actual criminal showed up one day as a visitor to speak with you

- ➤ your spouse were sent to prison for a crime you were sure they did not commit

- ➤ your spouse were on the run from the law and they wanted you to meet them and leave the country with them

- ➤ you could only have a liquid diet for the rest of your life

- ➤ you found an old, sealed, personal letter in the back of a dresser you bought from a yard sale – do you open it – what does it say

- ➤ you missed the last bus out of town for the holidays and nothing in the town would be open for four days

- ➤ someone you have never heard of names you in their will and what you are to receive shocks you

- ➤ a homeless relative dies and leaves you a million dollars

- ➤ your favorite aunt has been kidnapped and the kidnappers reached out to you and you are to tell NO ONE else or they will kill her

- no business transactions could be conducted on Sundays

- you were at the shore and just as you were about to walk into the water you saw shark fins appear from below the surface

- while out in your backyard you see smoke and then flames coming from your disabled neighbor's house

- you were asked to give the eulogy of a family member you did not like

- you are to receive a large inheritance, but first you must do something a little shady

- you had to 'ride the rails' to get back home

- you were in an airplane when you felt and heard a loud thump from outside the plane

➢ you found out your best friend had a very painful terminal illness – would you help end their life if they asked you to

➢ groundhog day happened in the fall to predict an early winter or longer fall

➢ your neighbor broke into your house and stole from you at gunpoint

➢ you had a rough week at work and were happy to finally get home on a Friday evening only to receive a devastating phone call that would turn your world upside down

➢ you were talked into going on a blind date and things went terribly, terribly wrong

- you were eating lunch with a good friend and she began to choke – would you know what to do

- a waiter spilled hot soup all over your new, and very expensive blouse

- a 30-year old murder, that a distant family member was believed to be involved in, was reopened after you finally thought things had calmed down and went back to normal

- you were asked to assist in a murder investigation

- you were at a friend's house playing a friendly card game when the place all of the sudden was raided by the police

- all the banks closed their doors and didn't give back any of the money to their account holders

- you were kidnapped in a foreign country

- your child were kidnapped and the ransom that they asked for was way more money than you had available – they gave you 72 hours to come up with it

- we could just talk to our computers and they would understand and do everything we asked them to do

- you were invited to a huge family reunion that hadn't taken place in over 50 years

- you suspect your neighbor of being the neighborhood thief

➤ you found out your new neighbors had a past they were trying to run away from

➤ your neighbors used their house to host 'swinger parties'

➤ you decided to open an animal rescue and all of the sudden people started dropping off animals in your yard

➤ one sunny morning you went out for a day hike on trails a mile or so from your house and about half way in you got caught in a downpour – so heavy was the rain that you could not see

➤ while walking along a new trail you lost your footing and slid down an embankment, twisting your ankle along the way

➢ you quit your job to start staying home with the kids only to go home and find out your spouse has just been fired

➢ you are crawling out onto the fire escape to escape a burning building and the metal stairs starts to pull away from the side of the building

➢ you are worried about your two year old who has yet to speak a work and take them to a specialist who tells you he is a mute

➢ you wake up in the hospital after a horrific car accident and find out you have lost your hearing and sight in one eye

➢ the means of human transportation is no longer done through road vehicles, but with flying vehicles (hover craft, helicopters, airplanes, etc.)

➢ your mother has been diagnosed with a mental illness and you need to decide if you can care for her at home or you need to put her in an institution that can care for her better than you

➢ milk were $20 a gallon

➢ you see an old lady slowly walking alongside a dangerous back road in a rain storm

➢ you are finally released from prison after serving a twenty year sentence for a crime you didn't commit and no one is there to pick you up

➢ you blacked out and when you woke up you were covered in blood and a dead body lay beside you with a knife sticking out of his chest – you can't remember a thing

- ➤ your husband's army unit is finally returning home from a yearlong deployment overseas – you are eagerly looking as each service member leaves the bus, but do not see your spouse anywhere

- ➤ your elderly parent has been mugged and beaten badly and the local police are not doing anything to try and find the perpetrator – do you take the law into your own hands

- ➤ you are playing a game at a family gathering and you see one member cheating – what do you do

- ➤ all the witnesses to the crime that was committed against you start slowly disappearing

- you are asked to testify against a well-known, and ruthless crime boss – do you

- you start having flashbacks of a crime you don't remember

- you are at a big family wedding and you think it is odd when you see the bride slip into a taxi out from – only to later see the groom (not your family's side) is left standing at the altar

- you are shopping for your nephew's birthday gift when several gunmen enter the mall and start shooting

- you find out a secret recording was made of a very private and personal conversation you had with your therapist

- you are on a family vacation aboard a cruise ship and it starts to sink

- a stranger walks up to you and starts talking to you like they've known you for years

- you had been home for a week unable to go out due to illness and just when you think you may be getting well enough to go to the store a big snow storm hits and doesn't let up for days leaving you stuck inside for another week – what do you do

- you are at the court house to file paperwork when a criminal, there for a trial, breaks free from the police and bolts towards the door – the one you are standing in front of – what do you do

- no food were perishable, but lasted forever

➢ you have been feeling weird for days and then you see him – a co-worker that just happens to be in the shadows no matter where you go

➢ your neighbor tells you that you kid damaged their car throwing rocks at it – you kid, however, swears they didn't do it but won't tell the name of the kid who did

➢ you get one dying wish fulfilled – what would that wish be

➢ during a blood test to see if you're a match to donate a kidney to your sibling, you find out the two of you are not related at all

➢ you found a stray dog sitting on your porch when you got home from work

➢ you had planned a huge 50th wedding anniversary for your parents and the night before the event your father dies in his sleep

➢ you found out someone was impersonating you

➢ you are a reporter assigned to investigate police corruption in your small town

➢ your marriage of 22 years is ending

➢ you are walking by a politically rally in front of your local capitol and things suddenly turn violent

➢ you are just about to go to bed when you hear a knock at your door – you open the door only to see the sister you haven't seen in almost 20 years

ADD YOUR OWN WHAT-IF QUESTIONS:

➢ _____

_____

➢ _____

_____

➢ _____

_____

➢ _____

_____

➢ _____

_____

➢ _____

_____

➢ _____

_____

➢ _____

_____

➢ _____

_____

➢ _____

_____

➢ _____

_____

➢ _____

_____

➢ _____

_____

➢ _____

_____

➢ _____

_____

➢ _____

_____

➢ _____

➢

➢

➢

➢

➢

➢

➢

➢

- _____

  _____

- _____

  _____

- _____

  _____

- _____

  _____

- _____

  _____

- _____

  _____

- _____

  _____

- _____

  _____

- _____

Note To Readers

Thank you for taking this journey with me. I wish you many happy days of writing and hope with this years' worth of writing prompts you will have no trouble coming up with a daily writing habit.
If you enjoyed these prompts please share your love for the Writing Prompts & Exercises books! Word-of-mouth is vital for an author to succeed.

If you enjoyed "What If…", please leave a review at Amazon, even if it's just a sentence or two. Your reviews make a ton of difference and are so appreciated.

For updates on the next book in this series and to be the first to hear about all of my other works, sign up for my **newsletter at janmariekelly.com** (***Note: your email will never be shared, and you can unsubscribe at any time.)

Also, feel free to email me at janmariepublishing(at)gmail(dot)com . I do answer each and every email – unless you're spamming me (LOL!).

You can connect and hang with me on <u>facebook</u> or drop by my website at **janmariekelly.com**

Books List

Thank you for taking this journey with me. If you enjoyed "What If…" please be sure to check out the other books in the Writing Prompts & Exercises series:

CURE WRITER'S BLOCK

Cure Writer's Block - Surely even the most prolific writer will not use all the prompts in this book.

JOURNALING PROMPTS:

Journaling Prompts - If you're a journaler who wants to know the secrets to a great journal and how to never run out of ideas then this is the book for you.

Until we meet again… Happy Writing.

www.ingramcontent.com/pod-product-compliance
Lightning Source LLC
Chambersburg PA
CBHW062341290526

45794CB00005B/2073